TABLE OF CONTENTS

THE BOOK OF LIFE

The Collected Wisdom of Dr. G. Christopher Berry

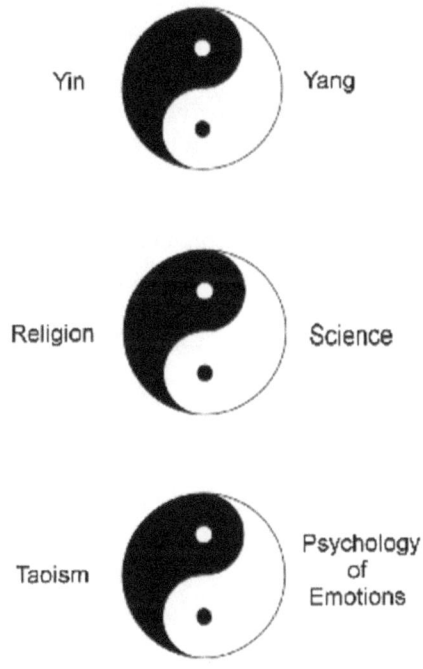

G. CHRISTOPHER BERRY PH.D.

ISBN: 1479188387

ISBN 13: 9781479188383

Library of Congress Control Number: 2012916851
CreateSpace Independent Publishing Platform
North Charleston, SC

FORWARD

I am a Psychologist who just happens to be a practicing Taoist and these are the most important things I have learned in my personal and professional life. These are the principles that I live my life by and this is what I teach clients who come to me for help. Some of what is contained within is common sense that needs to be repeated, other principles are the product of my work in the psychology of emotions over the last 30 years and are available nowhere else, some are my interpretation of ancient Taoist principles that are relevant to our world today and some are simply my prescriptions for a better world based on my experiences as a Psychologist. These are things that everyone should know about themselves and their world if they want to live a better life and help others have a better life too.

I have tried to be as concise as possible yet still be clear, there is no need for extra words. These are simple principles that almost everybody can understand. Like the Taoist sage, I share these bits of wisdom I have gleaned over the course of my lifetime with you. They are my gift to you so that you may make your life what you want it to be.

LESSON 1

LEARN

There is a purpose to life. It is not to acquire or attach ourselves to worldly things. It is not to enjoy the many varied and wonderful experiences of this world. And it is not to create more life for no purpose other than our own self-gratification, with little regard or responsibility for the life we create.

We are born and visited upon this planet to learn. Each receives their assigned tasks to accomplish in this lifetime. By their successes and failures each is judged upon their life's end.

Those who are successful move on to new tasks in the next life and benefit from their successes. Those who fail are sentenced to live out the rest of this life, and the next, in the sorrow and confusion of their failure, until they learn the tasks assigned to them.

So it is required of all human beings to learn from their own mistakes, to gather wisdom where they might-in success and failure and to accomplish the tasks mandated by heaven so that we all may someday ascend to sit with the Immortals.

LIFE

Life is a puzzle you put together piece by piece over time. Each question you ask and find the answer for reveals one piece of the puzzle. We take each answer where we find it, for there is some degree of truth in everything we experience.

Each succeeding answer you find brings the image of something hidden beneath closer to view, until such time that you know with certainty that the image hidden from view is a picture of you.

LESSON 3

SERENITY

Sooner or later everybody runs up against an obstacle that they cannot seem to conquer. When this occurs it is an indication that we have something new to learn.

Most of us try to change the situation first. Only when we learn we cannot change it do we realize we must learn to accept it.

We find serenity when we have the wisdom to know the difference between what we can change and what we must learn to accept.

UNDERSTANDING I

The only way we change is by understanding ourselves. The only way we change the world is by understanding others. In order to understand others, you must first understand yourself. In order to change the world, you must first change yourself.

UNDERSTANDING II

You cannot change what you do not understand.

LESSON 6

UNDERSTANDING III

To understand another person, first ask yourself, if I was in the situation of the person I am trying to understand, how would I feel?

Identify and name the feeling the other person is feeling. Remember situations in your life in which you experienced that same or a similar feeling. Even if it was in a different situation, the emotion you share feels the same to each of you.

Use your best imagination to create what it would feel like if what had happened to the other person had actually happened to you. Allow yourself to feel that feeling just as if it had happened to you.

Understand that, as bad as you feel, it may not even be close to how bad the other person feels. Then understand that what that person is feeling like, at that very moment, is a natural and normal reaction to what happened to them.

Now imagine what you would have to think and believe in order to feel what the other person is feeling. Thinking and believing what they would think and believe, and feeling what they are feeling, ask yourself: Is it any wonder that they do what they do?

Now take it a step further. Imagine what it would feel like to feel this way day after day, week after week, year after year. Now you have the best understanding of what it feels like to be another person you have ever had.

Do this for every person you meet. Soon you begin to understand why we have so much work to do to improve our world.

LESSON 7

BALANCE

Balance is perhaps the most important principle in the known universe. Balance is necessary in all things.

All things are paired with their opposite. Together they make the two extremes.

Health is always to be found in the middle.

LESSON 8

GROWTH

That which is not growing is dying.

Movement is the nature of life. That which is not moving forward is regressing backwards.

Of this you have no choice. You cannot return to that which you were. You can only move forward through growth to a better place yet unknown to you, to that which you will become.

LESSON 9

HEALTH

Health is the ability to meet your physical, mental, emotional and spiritual needs without interfering with other people's attempts to do the same.

LESSON 10

ILLNESS

Illness is the presence of intense emotions that get in the way of your attempts to be healthy.

Generally speaking, fear and anger, or other intense emotions of any kind, that grow too large and occupy too much of your time, constitute an issue or problem that would classify you as having a mental or emotional disorder.

Lesson 11

INTELLIGENCE

Intelligence is the ability to see patterns in the world and to be able to infer cause and effect.

Be like a scientist in your daily life. Look for patterns in the world. Form a hypothesis about what is creating those patterns. Test your hypothesis to see if you were right. Base your actions on facts that you deduce through reason and intelligence.

LESSON 12

PROBLEMS

A problem is a sign that you need to change yourself or the world.

Problems do not get better by themselves. Every problem should be followed by action to correct it.

It usually takes a concerted effort over an extended period of time to make major changes to yourself or your world.

The amount of time it takes to solve your issue or resolve your problem is proportional to the size of the problem and the amount of time that the problem or issue has existed in your life.

There are no free lunches. It takes work to improve your life.

L E S S O N 1 3

NEEDS

What any person needs is biologically and psychologically determined by evolution. Most people believe in a hierarchy of needs that begins with the lowest or most basic of physiological and psychological needs and advances upwards to higher needs that only become apparent when the lower needs are met.

These needs guide our behavior by creating wants and desires. Most people have problems because they misunderstand what their needs are trying to tell them to do and they try to meet those needs by fulfilling unrelated or incorrect desires.

Unhealthy people become trapped when they become confused about what is necessary to satisfy their needs. This will often lead to addictions and other unhealthy behavior. It occurs because core needs are not being met.

Once a need is met it will go away until another need is created. Healthy individuals have an ongoing series of wants and desires which, when satisfied, cause the underlying need to go away until some situation creates another need.

LESSON 14

MISSING PIECES

Most people are the walking wounded. They have a piece missing from their lives they don't know how to fill because, their parents did not teach them how to fill it.

No matter how hard they try to fill that missing piece it is never good enough because they are mistaken about what they are missing.

When you find that missing piece and learn how to give it to yourself, then you can learn to love yourself for who you are.

LESSON 15

CONTROL

The amount of control you desire over another person's life, is in inverse proportion to the amount of control you feel you have over your own life.

EMOTIONS I

Emotions are biology's adaptive mechanisms. They are a non-verbal language between your brain and your body in the form of an impulse to change your self or your world.

By denying, ignoring, repressing or suppressing your emotions you fail to adapt to your surroundings and problems occur.

Your goal must be to learn how to express those emotions in a healthy manner that will in time, lead to success and happiness.

LESSON 17

EMOTIONS II

Emotions should flow through us like a brook or stream, from the innermost parts of your animal being, driving you into action that changes your world for the better.

Your actions can be either healthy or unhealthy. Actions are healthy when they help you to meet your needs while allowing other people to do the same.

Your actions are unhealthy when they do not help you to meet your needs or they get in the way of another person's attempts to do the same.

Unhealthy behavior creates negativity in the world which is then multiplied many times over to many different people.

Attempts to ignore, deny, repress or suppress your emotions, or stop the natural flow of your emotions in any way will, over time, create illness and disease.

L E S S O N 1 8

EMOTIONS III

Every emotion has a purpose. Its purpose is to help you to adapt to your world. When you ignore, deny, repress or suppress your emotions, your world does not change and you create problems for yourself and others.

When ignored, denied, repressed or suppressed, emotions grow in intensity until they appear too big to control and they interfere with your daily functioning.

LESSON 19

EMOTIONS IV

You do not have a choice whether you feel an emotion or not, but you do have the choice of how you respond to it. You can choose to ignore, deny, repress or suppress it, which will cause pain in the future, or you can choose to express it in a negative manner which will cause pain in the present.

The wisest choice is to express your emotion in a healthy or positive manner, at the time it occurs. This will resolve your problem and reduce the probability that you will ever have to experience the same negative emotion in a similar situation again in the future.

RESOLVING EMOTIONS

In order to resolve an emotion, first recognize what you are feeling and "name" it. Accept the feeling as your own, as coming from you, without making judgments about yourself or your feelings as being bad or wrong.

Understand and acknowledge that no matter how unpleasant, or distasteful, or how much it hurts, it is a normal part of the human experience and it will not kill you to feel it. Most importantly, understand it has a purpose for you in this situation, and without it you cannot truly be successful or happy.

Allow yourself to "feel" the feeling. With intense feelings, you may need the help and support of someone you love or trust, or perhaps a professional beside you to keep you safe while you let yourself experience your emotions.

Identify what the feeling is telling you to do, without censoring or judging it. It hurts no one to simply acknowledge what you feel like doing, because you don't have to do it.

Use your intellect and reasoning to choose the best possible, socially acceptable behavior, that will allow you to do what your feeling is telling you to do, without causing hurt or harm to yourself or another person.

Then express the behavior you choose. Allow your behavior to change your situation. You cannot always predict or control how others will respond and you must accept how they react to your expression of emotion.

When you have done this correctly, the emotion created by your unique situation will go away.

LAWS OF EMOTIONS

Everyone has emotions and everyone has the potential to experience all emotions. We have no choice or control over whether we feel any emotion and all human beings have the potential to experience every emotion known. Most people will experience every emotion at some time during their life, depending upon the specific situations they are in.

Emotions must be expressed. Emotions must be allowed to do what they were meant to do. When emotions are not expressed, they remain with us until we either die, or learn how to "resolve" them.

Emotions have a purpose. Every emotion is created by our body for a specific purpose. That purpose is simply to change the situation we are in that created the emotion in the first place, and thus ensure our psychological and biological survival.

Emotions seek balance. Extreme emotions are the result of extreme life circumstances. When the true purpose of the emotion is understood and the emotion is resolved, our emotions will return to a state of equilibrium that defines "psychological health."

FEELINGS

ABANDONED, ADEQUATE, ADAMANT, ADMIRING, AFFECTIONATE, AFRAID, AGONY, AGITATED, ALIENATED, ALMIGHTY, AMBIVALENT, ANGRY, ANNOYED, ANTAGONISTIC, ANXIOUS, APATHETIC, APPREHENSIVE, ASHAMED, ASTOUNDED, AWED, BAD, BAFFLED, BEAUTIFUL, BETRAYED, BEWILDERED, BITTER, BLISSFUL, BOLD, BORED, BRAVE, BRIGHT, BURDENED, CALM, CAPABLE, CAPTIVATED, CHALLENGED, CHARMED, CHEATED, CHEERFUL, CHILDISH, CLEAR, CLEVER, CLOSED, COLD, COMBATIVE, COMPASSIONATE, COMPETITIVE, CONDEMNED, CONFIDENT, CONFUSED, CONSPICUOUS, CONTEMPTUOUS, CONTENTED, CONTRITE, CRUEL, CRUSHED, CULPABLE, DECEITFUL, DEFEATED, DELIGHTED, DESIROUS, DESPAIR, DESPERATE, DESTRUCTIVE, DETERMINED, DIFFERENT, DIFFIDENT, DIMINISHED, DISAPPOINTED, DISCONTENTED, DISCOURAGED, DISDAINFUL, DISGUSTED, DISMAYED, DISTRACTED, DISTURBED, DOMINATED, DIVIDED, DUBIOUS, EAGER, ECSTATIC, ELECTRIFIED, EMBARRASSED, EMPTY, ENCHANTED, ENCOURAGED, ENERGETIC, ENERVATED, ENJOY, ENVIOUS, ESTRANGED, EVIL, EXASPERATED, EXCITED, EXHAUSTED, EXPOSED, FASCINATED, FAWNING, FEARFUL, FLUSTERED, FOCUSED, FOOLISH, FRANTIC, FREE, FRIGHTENED, FRUSTRATED, FULL, FURIOUS, FURY, FUTILE, GAY, GLAD, GLOOMY, GOOD, GRATEFUL, GREEDY, GRIEF, GROOVY, GUILTY, GULLIBLE, HAPPY, HATE, HEAVENLY, HELD, HELPFUL, HELPLESS, HIGH, HOMESICK, HONORED, HORRIBLE, HUMOROUS, HURT, HYSTERICAL, IGNORED, IMMORTAL, IMPOSED UPON, IMPOTENT, INFATUATED, INFURIATED, INHIBITED, INSECURE, INSPIRED, INSATIABLE, INTIMIDATED, ISOLATED, JEALOUS(Y), JOYOUS, JUMPY, KINKY, KIND, KEEN, LACONIC, LAZY, LECHEROUS, LEFT OUT, LICENTIOUS, LIVID, LONELY, LONGING, LOUD, LOVING (LOVE), LOVED, LOW, LUSTFUL, MAD, MALICIOUS, MALIGNED, MAUDLIN, MEAN, MELANCHOLY, MISERABLE, MOODY, MUFFLED, MYSTICAL, NAUGHTY, NERVOUS, NICE, NIGGARDLY, NOSTALGIC, NUMB, NUTTY, OBNOXIOUS, ODD, ON DISPLAY, OPPOSED, OPPRESSED, OUTRAGED, OVERWHELMED, PAIN, PANICKED, PARSIMONIOUS, PATIENT, PEACEFUL, PERCEIVED, PERPLEXED, PERSECUTED, PETRIFIED, PITY, PLAYFUL, PLEASANT, PLEASED, PLUSH, PRECARIOUS, PRESSURED, PRIM, PRISSY, PROUD, PULLED, PUZZLED, QUARRELSOME, QUEER, RAGE, RAPTURE, REFRESHED, REJECTED, RELAXED, RELIEVED, REMORSE(FUL), RESENTFUL, RESIGNED, RESTLESS, REVERENT, REWARDED, RIGHTEOUS, ROUGH, SAD, SATED, SATISFIED, SCARED, SCREWED UP, SECURE, SENSITIVE, SERVILE, SETTLED, SEXY, SHAKY, SHOCKED, SHY, SILENCED, SILLY, SKEPTICAL, SMOOTH, SMOTHERED, SNEAKY, SOFT, SOLEMN, SORROWFUL, SPITEFUL, SPONGE, STARTLED, STINGY, STRANGE, STRANGLED, STUFFED, STUNNED, STUPEFIED, STUPID, SUFFERING, SURE, SUPPRESSED, SYMPATHETIC, TALKATIVE, TEMPTED, TENACIOUS, TENUOUS, TENSE, TENTATIVE, TERRIBLE, TERRIFIED, THREATENED, THWARTED, TIGHT, TIMID, TOUCHED, TREMBLING, TRIUMPHANT, TROUBLED, TRUSTING, UGLY, UNDERSTANDING, UNEASY, UNSETTLED, UNSTEADY, USED, VAGUE, VACILLATING, VEXED, VICTORIOUS, VIOLENT, VEHEMENT, VENGEFUL, VITAL, VITALITY, VULNERABLE, VIVACIOUS, WARM, WICKED, WEEPY, WONDERFUL, WORRY(IED), ZANY, ZAPPED

LESSON 23

TRIPLE BONUS

There are a finite number of things that we must learn in this world. When we learn to resolve a difficult emotion, we have learned one more thing on the list.

When we express our emotions in a healthy manner, we accomplish three things for our benefit and the benefit of the world.

We resolve an emotion in us and hence it goes away;

We learn how to deal with other similar emotions in the future, therefore improving our life, and;

We provide feedback to others, which they can use to improve their life.

A triple bonus: We benefit, others benefit and the world benefits from our decision to confront our own emotions.

PURIFYING THE WORLD

When tragedy besets us, or we experience trauma or pain as a result of something that happened to us in our life, we have the choice to either pass that pain on to others, or through hard work and diligence turn that pain into something that benefits ourselves and others.

To turn our pain into that which benefits others is what is known as purifying the world. Do this so that others do not have to go through what you had to go through.

PERFECTIONISM I

Rather than strive to be perfect and fail, strive to do the best that you can do, as much as you can do. Then there is no guilt and no remorse.

Over time it gets easier and easier until it becomes natural. When this happens you know you have grown.

PERFECTIONISM II

Perfectionism is a curse we inherited from parents who did not love us unconditionally.

LESSON 27

BURDENS

Carry your burden well. Be brave, but be honest.

FREE WILL

We are not free until the time we realize we have a choice in how to respond. Until that time we are no different from animals we keep.

Once we understand we have a choice of actions we become free and can choose the best course of action. This is what makes an individual a human being.

LESSON 29

HONESTY

Few people will ever know the joy of being completely honest yet compassionate and caring.

LESSON 30

HABITS

Bad habits are like a train speeding down the track in the wrong direction. In order to break a bad habit, you must first stop the speeding train. Then you must turn the train in the right direction and begin it slowly moving again. All of this takes time and effort. Bad habits are addictions. Good habits are healthy behavior.

EFFORT I

It doesn't matter how hard you try-as long as you try as hard as you can.

LESSON 32

EFFORT II

It matters how hard you try. People who put in little effort get little in return. Those who work as hard as they can are rewarded.

Most people are too impatient to recognize the results of their effort.

LESSON 33

SUCCESS

The surest way to success is to put one foot in front of the other, step after step, until you achieve your goal.

LESSON 34

GOALS I

Learn to love your goals no matter how difficult to achieve. Search out all possible benefits and costs and learn to love each as best you can. When you accomplish this you will have accomplished your goals.

GOALS II

You most often must fight to achieve your goals. If it comes easily, chances are it has little worth to you.

It is precisely because it is rare and difficult to achieve that it has great worth.

SIMILARITIES

Instead of looking at another person and asking yourself how are they different from you, try looking at that person and asking yourself how are they the same as you. What do they have in common with you as a member of the human race?

WORDS

Words are powerful. Words create our reality. They are the means by which we communicate with others and the way we understand and create our world.

LESSON 38

REALITY

There are two types of reality. The first and foremost is objective reality. This is what is real independent of how it is seen by yourself or others.

Objective reality exists but it is not available to human beings because of each humans propensity to distort reality according to their own experiences and desires.

The second type of reality is personal reality. Your personal reality is what is real to you. It is real to you because you choose to believe in it.

When you choose to believe in other than your traditional way of thinking, you open yourself up to new realities.

MEDITATION

Words have power. The things that you say to yourself over and over create your own reality.

By turning off those words through the many and varied forms of meditation and stillness, you can see the world from a different perspective.

Meditation gives us a choice. You do not have to continue to allow yourself to be drained by the fast and noisy pace of today's world.

Through meditation you have the opportunity to hear the subtle voices coming from your heart. There is much value to be found in hearing the subtle.

COSTS & BENEFITS

There are costs and benefits (Yin & Yang) to every choice we make. Those things which we normally associate with good have costs. Those things we normally associate as bad have benefits.

When choosing a course of action you must consider both the benefits and costs of each option available to you before making a decision.

LESSON 41

SELF-AWARENESS

Self-awareness is the crucial first step to understanding and changing your self and your world.

Not only must you become aware of those around you, you must also become aware of what you think, feel and do because, that is the only way you will ever be able to change it.

LESSON 42

CHANGE

Make change a friend.

PRACTICE

Reach, Practice, Learn.

This is the road to success.

PATIENCE I

Be patient.

It takes time for one to accumulate the benefits of good action.

PATIENCE II

Many people fail to learn because they are too impatient to recognize the consequences of their actions.

LESSON 46

RELATIONSHIPS

A healthy relationship is a relationship between equals. Any inequality in a relationship will eventually lead to problems.

The healthiest relationships occur between independent and self-sufficient individuals who do not need a relationship but choose to become involved in a relationship because it enhances their life.

COMMUNICATION

Communication is the key to successful relationships, whether they be between a husband and a wife, a parent and a child, an employer and an employee or two friends. Without successful communication, needs do not get met, and the relationship fails.

LESSON 48

GROWING

If you do not grow together in a relationship, you will grow apart.

L E S S O N   4 9

OPPOSITES

It is possible to have two diametrically opposed feelings (like Love & Hate) about somebody or something, at the same time.

LESSON 50

CONSISTENCY

Be consistent.

How are others expected to know you except by your word.

Say what you mean, mean what you say, or don't say it at all.

LESSON 51

EXPECTATIONS

Prepare for every eventuality but do not expect any outcome more than another.

LESSON 52

DOING

Do not try, simply do.

The person who tries leaves the door open for failure.

Trying becomes an excuse for not succeeding

LESSON 53

BENDING

Bend and not break. Give a little and do not be so rigid.

CHILDREN

We have a responsibility to the unborn children who would inhabit our world: To not bring them into a world where they will have little or no chance of meeting their needs, of having a satisfying life, or the opportunity to grow and learn what they need to in this life.

Our responsibility to them is a million times greater than our wishes to have children of our own. More than good intentions are required to provide a loving and fitting place for the children that we bear.

Simply because it was good enough for us does not mean our children should have to go through what we had to go through. If we have not prepared ourselves for the great responsibility of having children then we are incapable of doing right by the children that we bear.

Never bring a child into this world until you fully understand what happened to you as a child and you are absolutely sure that you will not pass on the hurt that you experienced to your children.

Recognize that it is out of love, perhaps the greatest love, that a parent can have for a child to not bring them into a world in which they will experience a life of pain and suffering.

Together we can put an end to the cycle of pain and suffering on this planet if we simply choose not to perpetuate it by having children we are incapable of properly providing for because we have failed to resolve our own problems.

Lesson 55

IMMORTALITY

Enlightenment has many levels. The achievement of immortality is a step by step process over the course of a lifetime, but all people benefit from a virtuous life no matter what their level of attainment.

LESSON 56

EXERCISE

Exercise moves the blood. The blood moves the chi. When chi is moved the muscles and the tissues are rejuvenated.

Unnecessary body fat holding unresolved emotions is lost and emotional blockages to the movement of the chi in the tissues and the muscles are removed.

LESSON 57

FEEDBACK

We have a moral and social responsibility to provide feedback to others about how their actions affect us. Without that feedback others can and will make incorrect decisions about how to deal with us and the world.

By providing constructive, beneficial feedback about how others impact our life, we provide the opportunity for them to understand how their actions affect others, and thus help them to choose the proper course of action that will benefit not just themselves but others.

LESSON 58

LAWS

The highest laws are not written, they exist in our hearts. They can be heard by those who still the noise of this world long enough to hear them.

MORALITY

Morality does not come from God. Morality comes from an understanding of your relationship with your planet, with an understanding of your relationship with other human beings and with an understanding of your relationship with yourself.

Do not look to another, even a God to tell you what is right and wrong. You must look to your heart for the understanding you seek.

MOVEMENT

Move forward. You cannot go back,
and you cannot stay where you are.

LESSON 61

NOT-DOING

In times of chaos and strife, it is time for the not-doing. In not-doing, we allow the great balance to return. In not-doing Yin and Yang complement each other to make the one.

PERSPECTIVE

When you say that you don't understand another's behavior, you are making a statement about your inadequacies rather than the appropriateness or health of the other person's behavior.

No matter how strange or unusual another's behavior may seem to you, it most often makes sense to them. Your inability to see the situation from their perspective makes it appear that their behavior does not make sense.

COMPETITION

Instead of competing against others, compete with yourself. You are the best competition you will ever have.

PRIMORDIAL-CAUSE

The primordial cause created all things and gave birth to existence. It endowed all existence with being and gave it a way to replicate itself.

LESSON 65

PAIN I

Doctors know that physical pain is a sign of physical problems in the body. Psychologists know that emotional or mental pain is the sign of emotional problems in the body.

Emotional pain is a sign that you have a problem or issue that needs to be dealt with. Ignoring it or pretending it is not there may remove the problem and pain from your conscious awareness for a short time, but it does not make the problem, or the pain it causes, actually go away.

Only confronting the problem and resolving the emotion can make the problem and the pain go away for good.

LESSON 66

PAIN II

Walk steadily towards the pain.

Stop only in consideration of those around you or to rest. Let nothing deter you from your quest.

LESSON 67

HAPPINESS

Seek not happiness, but rather peace and tranquility. Happiness is an intense emotion that is situational in nature and cannot be sustained in the long term.

Peace and tranquility can last an eternity. Those who know it find it deep and profound, encompassing all without the need for more. All other emotions are transient as they are part of the self.

L E S S O N 6 8

RESPONSIBILITY

Be responsible,

Honor your word,

Undo what has been done,

Put back what has been taken

and,

leave the world in a better place.

BODY

Your body is the vessel that holds your spirit. In order to effectively purify your spirit you must first perfect your body as a vessel for that spirit.

QUESTIONS

You can find the answer to any question you can't answer, by simply asking it of yourself, sincerely and passionately over and over.

You must, however, be open to all forms of answers and must be smart enough to recognize the answer when it appears.

Over time, if you follow this guide, you will find the answer to any question you desire.

LESSON 71

BEING I

Being is a word we use to describe our existence in this life. Non-being is a word we use to describe our existence in the next non-life.

Existence is a word we use to describe our being in this world, non-existence are the words we use to describe our non-being in the next world.

BEING II

Thought is the spark of being.